THE OUTPOUR

Foundations of Prophetic Ministry in the 21st Century

THE OUTPOUR

FOUNDATIONS OF PROPHETIC MINISTRY IN THE 21ST CENTURY

Michelle McClain-Walters

This book or parts thereof may not be reproduced in any form, stored in a retrieval system, or transmitted in any form by any means—electronic, mechanical, photocopy, recording, or otherwise—without prior written permission of the publisher, except as provided by United States of America copyright law.

The Outpour by Michelle McClain-Walters
All rights reserved.
Copyright © 2018 by Michelle McClain-Walters.

Visit the author's website at www.michellemcclainwalters.com
Visit the book's website at www.yourwealthyplace.com

All scriptures used in this study guide were taken from the New King James Version®. Copyright © 1982 by Thomas Nelson. Used by permission. All rights reserved.

Where noted the Amplified Bible (AMP), Copyright © 2015 by The Lockman Foundation, La Habra, CA 90631. All rights reserved. For Permission To Quote information visit http://www.lockman.org/

Instructional Designer: Regine Jean-Baptiste, !Impact Course Developers

ISBN-13: 978-1-7256390-5-8
ISBN-10: 1-7256-3905-X

While the author has made every effort to provide accurate Internet addresses at the time of publication, neither the publisher nor the author assumes any responsibility for errors or for changes that occur after publication.

17 18 19 20 21 — 9 8 7 6 5 4 3 2 1

Printed in the United States of America

"And it shall come to pass afterward
That I will pour out My Spirit on all flesh;
Your sons and your daughters shall prophesy,
Your old men shall dream dreams,
Your young men shall see visions.
And also on My menservants and on My maidservants
I will pour out My Spirit in those days.
~ Joel 2: 28-29

TABLE OF CONTENTS

Introduction 1
Lesson 1: Prophetic Ministry in the 21st Century 3
    God's Outpouring 4
    Biblical Foundation for Prophecy 5
    Pursue Prophecy 10
    Lesson Reflections 11
Lesson 2: The Gift and Spirit of Prophecy 17
    Foundations to the Prophetic 18
    Office of the Prophet 19
    Gift of Prophecy 20
    Spirit of Prophecy 20
    Functions of the Office of the Prophet 20
    God's View of the Gift of Prophecy 21
    God's View of the Spirit of Prophecy 24
    Lesson Reflections 26
Lesson 3: Identifying the Call of the Prophet 31
    The Call of God 32
    Expectations of the Call 33
    Dimensions in a Prophet's Development 33
    Deals of the Call 35
    Your Message 36
    Your Vision 36
    Commissioning 37
    Lesson Reflections 39
Lesson 4: Roadblocks to Accuracy 45
    Dimension of Accuracy 46
    Roadblocks to Accurate Delivery 46
    Tips to Follow 50

    Lesson Reflections 52
Lesson 5: Seek to Excel in Prophecy 59
    Receiving Prophetic Words 60
    Receiving from the Spirit of God 61
    Prophesying to Believers 62
    The Prophetic Flow 64
    God Speaks 65
    Lesson Reflections 67
Lesson 6: The Role of the Prophet in the Local Church 73
    Set in the Church 74
    Positions for Prophets in the Church 74
    Bringing the Word of God to the Local Church 77
    Prophets of Breakthrough and Revival 78
    Lesson Reflections 80
About The Author 85
Answer Key 87

INTRODUCTION

Welcome to the Wealthy Place, a destiny mentorship academy where you will be equipped with the essential tools to fulfill your God-given assignment and receive the motivational support to walk out your destiny.

God is releasing His voice upon the earth. He wants to speak to you and through you as a gift of His Spirit. Embracing this Christian birthright will usher you to experience the outpour of God's Spirit, which will cause you to prophesy as a son or daughter of God. This course is designed to teach you the practical steps to operate in prophecy and how to understand the levels of prophetic ministry. The lesson notes and reflection journal questions found in this study guide, should be paired with the video teachings. You can access the online videos by visiting www.yourwealthyplace.com.

I pray that as you complete these course materials that a fresh outpouring of God's Spirit is released in your life. I declare the Spirit of God meets you with the confidence to hear God's voice for your life and empowers you to speak God's words in the lives of others. May the wind of the Holy Spirit fill you with the expression of God's heart for your life and for the lives of others.

Prophetess Michelle McClain-Walters
Founder of the Wealthy Place Destiny Academy
www.yourwealthyplace.com

LESSON 1

PROPHETIC MINISTRY IN THE 21ST CENTURY

And it shall come to pass in the last days, says God,
That I will pour out of My Spirit on all flesh;
Your sons and your daughters shall prophesy,
Your young men shall see visions,
Your old men shall dream dreams. ~ Acts 2:17

We are living in a time when God is pouring out His flesh on all sons and daughters to prophecy. In this lesson you will learn:

- Reasons for God outpouring through the Holy Spirit

- Biblical foundations for prophecy

- Why we should pursue prophecy

The Outpour

GOD'S OUTPOURING

Fill in the blanks as you watch the video teachings to complete the lesson notes.

1. We serve a God who speaks _____ and _____.

2. God speaks in many ways, and this is our _____ and _____.

3. A characteristic of the outpouring is that God wants a people who is walking in _____ to him to move in the same power Jesus walked in on earth.

4. This outpouring gives us access into the _____ of the Holy Spirit's activities.

5. This means that we can _____, _____, and _____ in the same power Jesus operated in on earth.

Walking in the realm of the prophetic is our birthright. It is the grace to be transformed!

6. The centerpiece of the outpouring of God's spirit is to _____.

*'And it shall come to pass in the last days, says God,
That I will pour out of My Spirit on all flesh;
Your sons and your daughters shall prophesy,
Your young men shall see visions,
Your old men shall dream dreams. ~ Acts 2:1*

7. If you are a son or daughter (a believer of Jesus Christ) and filled with the Holy Spirit you are _____ to operate in prophetic.

God is equipping the Body of Christ to hear His voice and to go out and get the harvest through prophecy.

BIBLICAL FOUNDATION FOR PROPHECY

*Now concerning spiritual gifts, brethren, I do not want you to be ignorant
~ 1 Corinthians 12:1*

1. To move in the spirit of God, we must come to a new place of _____ and _____.

   a. We don't operate in the gifts of the spirit because we are lacking knowledge about them.

b. We have a responsibility as sons and daughters to have an understanding .

that _____ and allows

us to operate in the spirit of God.

Pursue love, and desire spiritual gifts, but especially that you may prophesy.
~ 1 Corinthians 14:1

2. All the gifts of the spirit operate by _____, you

need to understand how much God loves you and that He has a love for mankind.

a. To operate in the fullness of everything God has for us, we have to start with

a _____.

b. Desire means to _____, _____

_____, and to go after something or someone.

"Delight yourself also in the Lord, And He shall give you the desires of your heart." ~ Psalm 37:4

c. Prophecy is hearing the _____ and the

_____ for your life, a situation, for your

generation, your nation, and even for your city. God wants to reveal his heart and

mind to us.

d. Prophecy is a _____ given by the

_____ to hear the voice of God and release it

to others.

e. We release God's _____ and _____ through prophecy.

But covet earnestly the best gifts. ~1 Corinthians 12:31a

3. The best gift of the Spirit is the _____.

   a. Covet means to _____, lust after, _____ and yarn for someone or something.

   b. You can covet the gift of prophecy.

"Therefore I remind you to stir up the gift of God which is in you through the laying on of my hands. For God has not given us a spirit of fear, but of power and of love and of a sound mind." ~ 2 Timothy 1:6-7

4. Stir up the gifts of the Spirit by being _____ that you at least have one of the gifts of the Spirit.

   a. Ask God to impart, activate, and _____ the gift of prophecy on the inside of you.

   b. Pray and ask the Lord to _____ you with the knowledge of His will and the gift of prophecy.

   c. Come to some activations.

   d. The enemy wants to stop believers from operating in the fullness of the gifts of the spirit by attacking us with the spirit of fear; but God has given us a spirit of

_____, _____,

and a _____.

You have the spirit of power, love, and a sound mind so stir up your faith to use the gifts of the Spirit!

Even so you, since you are zealous for spiritual gifts, let it be for the edification of the church that you seek to excel. ~ 1 Corinthians 14:12

5. Prophecy is given to the body of Christ and to _____ the church.

    a. Edify means to _____.

    b. We have to seek, to go after, _____, and to desire to prophesy.

    c. We want to seek ways to bless the church, by being excellent in the gifts of prophecy and the gifts of the spirit.

Do not quench the Spirit. ~1 Thessalonians 5:19

6. With _____ and _____,

you can quench the spirit of God.

a. God is releasing faith on the inside of you to move with the Spirit of God.

"Despise not the gift" ~ 1 Timothy 4:14a

7. The enemy can cause you to despise the gifts of the Spirit.

    a. Despise means to feel _____, to reject, or to _____.

    b. Prophets and prophecy were God's ideas. He knew the misnomers and mistakes that would cause us to have the tendency to _____ and despise the gift of prophecy, but we can't throw the baby out with bathwater just because of mistakes.

The prophetic realm is God's idea!

For though by this time you ought to be teachers, you need someone to teach you again the first principles of the oracles of God; and you have come to need milk and not solid food. ~ Hebrews 5:12

8. Exercise and use the gifts because:

    a. You can _____ or _____ the gifts.

Do not neglect the gift that is in you, which was given to you by prophecy with the laying on of the hands of the eldership. ~ 1 Timothy 4:14

9. We neglect the gift of God by not _____ or partnering with a spirit of _____. We attend to the gifts of the spirit by:

   a. Paying attention to the gifts and studying the God's word.

   b. Taking every scripture you can find as it relates to prophets and prophecy and studying and meditating on them.

Please note for Scripture bank, see Chapter 10 of the Prophetic Advantage book.

PURSUE PROPHECY

1. Christ _____ us to pursue prophecy.

2. When we pursue prophecy, it will bring great _____ _____ _____.

3. Prophecy will cause you to draw near to God and to understand how much God loves you and the whole world.

God is pouring out His Spirit and it will cause a generation to prophecy!

LESSON REFLECTIONS

After completing the video teachings, take a moment to reflect on the lesson using the following journal prompts.

1. We serve a God who speaks to us and through us. Take a moment to journal the last time you experienced God speaking to you and the last time you experienced God speaking through you. Why do you think the ability to hear God's voice is a promise and a birthright for all Christian believers?

2. To move in the spirit of God we must come to a new place of knowledge and understanding. What is a new revelation you gained concerning prophecy as you listened to this teaching?

3. As we cultivate hearing the voice of the Lord for ourselves, we can also grow in the ability to hear the voice of the Lord for others. Grab a partner and begin cultivating the voice of the Lord by listening and sharing with that person what God desires to communicate to him or her. Use the following activations to help you share God's voice with your partner.

Select one of the activations below. Take a moment to pray and ask God what to communicate to your partner concerning the topic. For example, if you selected the first topic, you would pray and ask, "God, what color does [insert partner's name] represent to You?" When you hear an answer, you would pray again and ask God, "Why? What does that mean?" Then you would share with the person what the Lord communicated to you. Now, choose one of the topics below and begin listening for God's voice.

    a. What color does this person represent to God?

    You represent _____ color to God because _____.

    b. What season does this person represent to God?

    You represent _____ season because _____.

    c. What room does this person represent to God?

    You represent _____room because _____.

Notes

The Outpour

LESSON 2

THE GIFT AND SPIRIT OF PROPHECY

And He Himself gave some to be apostles, some prophets, some evangelists, and some pastors and teachers, for the equipping of the saints for the work of ministry, for the edifying of the body of Christ
~ Ephesians 4:11-12

God is releasing His voice upon the earth and He wants a people that can understand the fullness of the gift of prophecy. In this lesson you will learn about the:

- Basics to the prophetic

- Nature of prophecy

- Levels of prophetic ministry

FOUNDATIONS TO THE PROPHETIC

Fill in the blanks as you watch the video teachings to complete the lesson notes.

1. The two natures or ways and expressions of prophecy is:

    a. Forthtelling which is _____ the heart and mind of God.

    b. Foretelling which is to speak in a level of _____, _____, to communicate the future, or to set the agenda of God.

2. The three levels of prophetic ministry is the:

    a. Office of the prophet which is the _____ _____ and also the ministry of Jesus.

    b. Gift of prophecy is the gift of the Holy Spirit _____ _____.

    c. Spirit of prophesy which is created in an atmosphere of _____ where it is easy to prophecy in the local church.

OFFICE OF THE PROPHET

And He Himself gave some to be apostles, some prophets, some evangelists, and some pastors and teachers, for the equipping of the saints for the work of ministry, for the edifying of the body of Christ
~ Ephesians 4:11-12

1. Prophets exist because we are still being _____

   _____.

2. Before Jesus ascended He took his mantle and separated it into five different pieces know as the:

   a. Office of the _____

   b. Office of the _____

   c. Office of the evangelist

   d. Office of the _____

   e. Office of the teacher

3. It is a gift and calling from God to operate in one of these _____ ascension gifts.

GIFT OF PROPHECY

1. The gift of prophesy is given by the _____ to those who desire it.

SPIRIT OF PROPHECY

And I fell at his feet to worship him. But he said to me, "See that you do not do that! I am your fellow servant, and of your brethren who have the testimony of Jesus. Worship God! For the testimony of Jesus is the spirit of prophecy."
~ Revelation 19:10

1. The spirit of prophesy is when the _____ is among believers.

2. When you come to worship gatherings the spirit of prophecy can rest upon you to _____ _____.

FUNCTIONS OF THE OFFICE OF THE PROPHET

1. The functions of the office of the prophet is to provide _____

for the local church.

2. Prophets bring _____ and rebuke.

3. They have the ability to _____

of God's judgments or blessings.

4. Prophets move in the strong levels of _____.

5. They move in the realm of illumination or _____.

of what God has to say to the church today.

6. Prophets lay foundations in the church.

7. They _____ spiritual gifts.

GOD'S VIEW OF THE GIFT OF PROPHECY

Pursue love, and desire spiritual gifts, but especially that you may prophesy. For he who speaks in a tongue does not speak to men but to God, for no one understands him; however, in the spirit he speaks mysteries. But he who prophesies speaks edification and exhortation and comfort to men. He who speaks in a tongue edifies himself, but he who prophesies edifies the church ~ 1 Corinthians 14:1-4

1. We prophesy to _____ the church.

2. The gift of prophecy operates in three realms:

    a. Edification

        i. Edify is an act of _____, to instruct,

and to _____, or to establish.

ii. One of the dimensions of the prophetic realm is to _____ _____.

iii. Prophecy is a spiritual tool we can use through our words to bring edification to someone else.

b. Exhortation

i. Exhort means to call someone to move into action, _____, _____, or to quicken too.

ii. Sometimes a word of exhortation can be a _____ _____.

iii. Holy Spirit on the inside of us is watching over our words to perform it.

c. Comfort

i. Comfort means to _____, to ease, to uphold the mind of someone depressed, or to _____ _____.

ii. Holy Spirit is known as the Comforter, He releases comfort by using vessels like us to speak words that will bring comfort to people.

For I know the thoughts that I think toward you, says the Lord, thoughts of peace and not of evil, to give you a future and a hope. ~ Jeremiah 29:11

3. When you begin moving in the realm of prophecy you begin releasing

   _____.

   How forceful are right words! ~ Job 6:25a

4. When you prophesy make sure you are releasing _____

   _____.

   'And it shall come to pass in the last days, says God,
   That I will pour out of My Spirit on all flesh;
   Your sons and your daughters shall prophesy,
   Your young men shall see visions,
   Your old men shall dream dreams. ~ Acts 2:17

5. When moving in prophecy it is a realm of edification, exhortation, and comfort to God's people with His words in your mouth.

God will use you as a mouthpiece to speak words of comfort, exhortation, and edification to others!

The Outpour

GOD'S VIEW OF THE SPIRIT OF PROPHECY

1. The greatest outpouring that God can release on a _____ _____ simultaneously is the spirit of prophecy.

When they came there to the hill, there was a group of prophets to meet him; then the Spirit of God came upon him, and he prophesied among them.
~ 1 Samuel 10:10

2. When the spirit of prophecy is in the atmosphere it:

    a. Turns your _____ and turns your

    _____.

        i. The spirit of prophecy is not resident. For example, when the spirit of prophecy came upon Saul it was not resident it was a _____ _____ that came upon him from God.

        ii. When you minister to God in worship, the spirit of prophecy comes upon you. Saul received a _____ because of the spirit of prophecy. When he prophesied he turned into a new man.

    b. Turns the heart and the nature of others.

One of the greatest ways we can testify of Jesus is when we release words of prophecy!

3. The spirit of prophecy resting upon us as we worship is to bring _____ and _____.

Having then gifts differing according to the grace that is given to us, let us use them: if prophecy, let us prophesy in proportion to our faith. ~ Romans 12:6

4. We operate in the spirit of prophecy when we worship according to the portion of our _____.

LESSON REFLECTIONS

After completing the video teachings, take a moment to reflect on the lesson using the following journal prompts.

1. Review the three levels of prophetic ministry. Take a moment to journal your past experiences with these different levels of the prophetic. Are your experiences most consistent with the office, gift, or spirit of prophecy?

2. We operate in the spirit of prophecy according to the portion of our faith. On the scale of 1-10 rate your level of faith. One represents the lowest of faith or no faith and ten represents an unyielding belief in God, where you can say "I believe God and see the manifestation of my faith daily." Why did you rate your faith using this number? What can you do to intentionally strengthen your faith?

3. As we cultivate hearing the voice of the Lord for ourselves, we can also grow in the ability to hear the voice of the Lord for others. Grab a partner and begin cultivating the voice of the Lord by listening and sharing with that person what God desires to communicate to him or her. Use the following activations to help you share God's voice with your partner.

Select one of the activations below. Take a moment to pray and ask God what to communicate to your partner concerning the topic. For example, image you selected the topic, "What color does your partner represent to God?" You would pray and ask, "God, what color does [insert partner's name] represent to You?" When you hear an answer, you would pray again and ask God, "Why? What does that mean?" Then you would share with the person what the Lord communicated to you. Now, choose one of the topics below and begin listening for God's voice.

    a. Ask God for an encouraging word to share with your partner. Why does God want to share that word with your partner?

    b. Ask God for a specific phrase that will resonate with your partner. Why does God want to communicate that phrase?

    c. Ask God for a meaningful street name for your partner. What does God want to communicate to your partner through this meaningful street name?

Notes

The Outpour

LESSON 3

IDENTIFYING THE CALL OF THE PROPHET

Then the word of the Lord came to me, saying:
"Before I formed you in the womb I knew you;
Before you were born I sanctified you;
I ordained you a prophet to the nations."
Then said I: "Ah, Lord God!
Behold, I cannot speak, for I am a youth."
But the Lord said to me:
"Do not say, 'I am a youth,'
For you shall go to all to whom I send you,
And whatever I command you, you shall speak.
Do not be afraid of their faces,
For I am with you to deliver you," says the Lord.
Then the Lord put forth His hand and touched my mouth,
and the Lord said to me:
"Behold, I have put My words in your mouth.
See, I have this day set you over the nations and over the kingdoms,
To root out and to pull down,
To destroy and to throw down,
To build and to plant."
Moreover the word of the Lord came to me, saying,
"Jeremiah, what do you see?"
And I said, "I see a branch of an almond tree." ~Jeremiah 1:4-11

Prophets are called since they were in their mother's womb. This call must be identified to be used for the glory of God. In this lesson you will learn about the:

- Prophet's call

- Expectations and training required for prophets

- Commissioning of a prophet

THE CALL OF GOD

Fill in the blanks as you watch the video teachings to complete the lesson notes.

1. The call of God is not like a _____, He call us before we were in our mother's womb.

2. Whatever you were called to do, when you came into your mother's womb God gave you _____.

3. The call of God is given by the _____.

4. It is up to us to _____ God's call by the power of God and by the Holy Spirit.

5. The prophet's office is given before we were in our mother's womb.

6. The call of God is an _____, started in the heart and mind of God and revealed by the Holy Spirit.

EXPECTATIONS OF THE CALL

For I know the thoughts that I think toward you, says the Lord, thoughts of peace and not of evil, to give you a future and a hope. ~ Jeremiah 29:11

1. God has an expectation for our lives and it is up to us to find it by getting before the _____.

2. We do not _____, _____, or _____ over anything – it is God who does the calling, setting, and appointing.

3. This does not mean we are rogue prophets and don't answer to anyone but God.

4. God sets prophets in the local _____ to be trained and commissioned.

DIMENSIONS IN A PROPHET'S DEVELOPMENT

There are three dimensions in a prophet's development.

1. The calling

   a. _____ through an audible voice, a dream, or from other people who can identify the call of God in your life.

b. Follow the draw and through the process of _____, God will identify you as a prophet.

2. God chooses the field where you are assigned.

   a. God is the one who gives you the _____ and _____ you where you are called.

   b. It is God who does the calling and chooses the prophet's assignment.

3. Appoints you to an office according to _____ and _____ for your life.

   a. When God ordains you He gives you the unction, anointing, and authority to function.

   b. Authority is the _____ or position to function.

   c. God will develop the _____ dimension in your life before you walk in the fullness of the office of the prophet.

   d. He doesn't just give _____ and _____. No, there is an unction and function that you have been assigned too, which means you need to be at the right place at the right time fulfilling the assignment of God.

   e. We need to let God cultivate in us the desire for the place we are assigned.

DEALS OF THE CALL

1. When you are being developed as a prophet, God will deal with the inadequacies or the _____ _____.

2. God will also deal with your _____ so that you have the capacity to carry out the call.

3. When God begins to speak to you about the call of God, He then _____ and _____ you.

4. In the place of training, God will deal with your fears, insecurities, and character, as He transforms you to carry out your assignment.

Your gift will get you to great platforms, but your character will get you to stand and remain on those platforms!

5. Fears try to eliminate our faith, therefore we have to let the Lord begin to equip us and deliver us so that our faith can jump over our fears.

YOUR MESSAGE

1. God will develop your message so you don't have to _____ _____.

2. Prophets bring messages of:

   a. _____

   b. _____

   c. Glory

   d. _____ and _____

Let the Lord develop your message!

3. Prophets should become confident and secure in the message that God has given them.

YOUR VISION

1. God will begin to recalibrate _____.

2. God will cause you to see _____ and _____ from His perspective.

3. Instead of looking from a low place or a human perspective, prophets are always

called to go to the high place to see things from God's perspective.

4. Prophets were often called to a high place to have their vision recalibrated, to see mankind, to see their city, and their nation from God's perspective.

5. Prophets will go to high places with God in worship and there, He will give them a _____.

Prophets don't speak from a place of opinion, they speak from the opinions of God.

COMMISSIONING

1. God wants to make you what _____.

2. The commissioning of God is a hard thing because we often don't see ourselves as God sees us.

3. If you have been called as prophet of the Lord, you must be trained during long seasons with the Lord and then _____ to be sent on assignment.

4. Credibility is not enough to hear the voice of God, we need _____ with God and man.

   a. God wants to give you credibility so that people can honor you and trust you.

When people trust you they will do what the word of the Lord is saying to do.

When you are set in the house of God, allow God to give you a message, and be determined to be a prophet sent from the presence of the Lord. God will give you credibility and believability. It is not enough to speak a word accurately it is important for people to believe us and to take action on God's directives.

LESSON REFLECTIONS

After completing the video teachings, take a moment to reflect on the lesson using the following journal prompts.

1. God is the one who gives you a calling and shows you where you are assigned. What do you believe God has called you to do? How did He reveal this calling to you? What has God been showing you lately about your calling? If you don't know where you are called or haven't received new visions lately, spend some time with God in prayer to inquire about your call.

2. In the place of training God deals with our fears, insecurities, and character, as He transforms us to carry out our assignment. What are some places that God has been dealing with you concerning yourself? How can you partner with the Holy Spirit to change those areas of insecurities, fear, or negative character traits?

3. As we cultivate hearing the voice of the Lord for ourselves, we can also grow in the ability to hear the voice of the Lord for others. Grab a partner and begin cultivating the voice of the Lord by listening and sharing with that person what God desires to communicate to him or her. Use the following activations to help you share God's voice with your partner.

Select one of the activations below. Take a moment to pray and ask God what to communicate to your partner concerning the topic. For example, image you selected the topic, "What color does your partner represent to God?" You would pray and ask, "God, what color does [insert partner's name] represent to You?" When you hear an answer, you would pray again and ask God, "Why? What does that mean?" Then you would share with the person what the Lord communicated to you. Now, choose one of the topics below and begin listening for God's voice.

    a. Ask God to communicate a key thing to you about your partner's past. Why does God want to share this particular point about your partner's past?

    b. Ask God to communicate a key thing to you about partner's present. Why does God want to share this particular point about your partner's present?

    c. Ask God to communicate some things about your partner's future. Why does God want to share this particular point about your partner's future?

Notes

The Outpour

LESSON 4

ROADBLOCKS TO ACCURACY

Behold, You desire truth in the inward parts,
And in the hidden part You will make me to know wisdom. ~ Psalm 51:6

If we are moving in the office of the prophet or just a believer that prophesies one of things we want to make sure is that we are speaking the word of God and that we are saying God's word in the exact expression of God. In this lesson you will learn about the:

- Dimension of accuracy

- Roadblocks we encounter to accurate prophetic delivery

- Most helpful tips for giving a prophetic word

The Outpour

DIMENSION OF ACCURACY

Fill in the blanks as you watch the video teachings to complete the lesson notes.

1. We can have right words, but the wrong expression of God's heart.

2. Accuracy means to be _____, _____, and to have the _____ of God.

3. To prophesy or to be a prophet is to speak the heart and mind of God.

4. The heart of God is the _____ or _____ of God.

Accuracy in the prophetic must contain the correct expression of God's heart!

ROADBLOCKS TO ACCURATE DELIVERY

Things that can stop your accuracy with the delivery of prophetic words:

1. To opinionated

    a. We think our opinion is _____.

    b. Don't speak your opinion.

    c. We stop speaking our opinions by seeking the Lord and not moving in

Foundations of Prophetic Ministry in the 21st Century

_____.

　d. Presumption is _____

_____

_____.

　e. Avoid presumption by spending time with God!

How precious also are Your thoughts to me, O God!
How great is the sum of them!
If I should count them, they would be more in number than the sand;
~ Psalm 139:17-18a

God has so many thoughts, we don't have to recycle or presume what God is thinking.

2. Prejudice

　a. We cannot have racial, gender, and cultural prejudices or we will miss the accuracy of the prophetic.

　b. Make sure you have a _____.

　c. The _____ of the prophetic ministry comes out of your heart.

A good man out of the good treasure of his heart brings forth good; and an evil man out of the evil treasure of his heart brings forth evil. For out of the abundance of the heart his mouth speaks. ~ Luke 6:45

Our greatest weapon is our heart and we want to have a pure heart that is purged of any level or expression of prejudices.

3. Rejection and the fear of rejection

   a. Rejection of the fear of rejection will have you speaking prophecies to get _____.

   b. Ask the Lord to heal and deliver you from rejection and the fear of rejection.

4. Fear of Man

   The fear of man brings a snare,
   But whoever trusts in the Lord shall be safe. ~ Prov 29:25

   a. The Greek word for snare means _____, _____, to put a ring in your nose.

   b. The fear of man will cause you to not prophesy without God's leading or to prophesy to _____ people.

5. Bitterness

   a. _____ can lead to bitterness and taint our flow.

   b. Make sure you are not angry. The enemy attacks prophets because he knows if he can get your heart, he can stop your accuracy.

6. Respecter of persons

   a. One of the dimensions of the prophet's office is likened to the high priest, who carried the breastplate with each jewel representing the twelve tribes of Israel.

   b. If you want to be accurate, you must be able to speak to the different tribes, _____ and even _____, because God is a God of the nations and of every ethnic background, church, and denomination.

7. Human Compassion

   a. We must have compassion on what _____.

   b. Make sure you do not prophesy out of _____, always go for the right expression.

Stick to your assignment!

The Outpour

8. To judgmental

   a. The grace on the New Testament prophet's life is to _____, not to point to everything that is wrong.

9. Judging by appearance

   a. Don't look at someone's _____.

   b. Ask the Lord what is on your heart and your mind for an individual.

   c. Don't let the appearance of someone _____ you.

10. Lust

    a. Lust is having a _____ desire for an object or a person.

    b. Prophets must guard their hearts from the lust of _____, _____, and _____.

TIPS TO FOLLOW

Here are some tips on how to ensure you are prophesying from a place of accuracy found in Psalm 51.

1. Have the right heart by desiring truth in your inmost parts by:

a. _____ Psalm 51.

b. Knowing the spirit of truth is the Holy spirit and He will give you truth

2. Have a heart to immediately repentant because:

a. Repentance makes it so that the wrong road will never become the right road.

   i. After repentance _____.

   ii. Ask God if there is any evil way in you to purge it, and God will hear your prayer.

   iii. Allow the Holy Spirit to _____.

Make it a daily practice to not have pride by repenting immediately when the Holy Spirit reveals an issue to you.

The Outpour

LESSON REFLECTIONS

After completing the video teachings, take a moment to reflect on the lesson using the following journal prompts.

1. Which of the roadblocks to prophecy has been the biggest hindrance for you in moving in the prophetic? How can you intentionally partner with the Holy Spirit to gain healing and deliverance from this roadblock?

2. Read over Psalm 51. Rewrite the Psalm in the form of a confession that you can use daily as you seek the truth of God in your heart.

The Outpour

3. As we cultivate hearing the voice of the Lord for ourselves, we can also grow in the ability to hear the voice of the Lord for others. Grab a partner and begin cultivating the voice of the Lord by listening and sharing with that person what God desires to communicate to him or her. Use the following activations to help you share God's voice with your partner.

Select one of the activations below. Take a moment to pray and ask God what to communicate to your partner concerning the topic. For example, image you selected the topic, "What color does your partner represent to God?" You would pray and ask, "God, what color does [insert partner's name] represent to You?" When you hear an answer, you would pray again and ask God, "Why? What does that mean?" Then you would share with the person what the Lord communicated to you. Now, choose one of the topics below and begin listening for God's voice.

    a. What movie character does this person represent to God?

    You represent _____ movie-character because _____.

    b. What comic book character does this person represent to God?

    You represent _____ comic book character because _____.

    c. What Bible character does this person represent to God?

    You represent _____ Bible character because _____.

Notes

The Outpour

LESSON 5

SEEK TO EXCEL IN PROPHECY

But as it is written:
"Eye has not seen, nor ear heard,
Nor have entered into the heart of man
The things which God has prepared for those who love Him."
~ 1 Corinthians 2:9

Everything in the kingdom of God is proactive. If you are going to walk in the fullness of God as a Christian believer you have to seek to excel. In this lesson you will learn how to:

- Receive a prophetic word

- Catch and obtain prophetic words from the Spirit of God

- Prophesy to believers

RECEIVING PROPHETIC WORDS

Fill in the blanks as you watch the video teachings to complete the lesson notes.

1. Without the Holy spirit we have a _____ to tap into and have greater understanding of the spiritual world.

2. We receive prophetic words though our senses. We have five natural senses just like we have five spiritual senses.

3. The way we catch prophecy is through our senses:

   a. Our spiritual eyes

       i. There is a dimension called the seer realm where we can _____ _____ _____.

       ii. The Holy Spirit will anoint your eyes like in 2 Kings 6 & 7 to see the things happening in the Spirit world that we cannot see with the naked eyes.

       iii. God can give you _____, _____, and _____ by anointing you and removing spirtuial scales from our eyes.

   b. Spiritual ears

       i. God can open up our spiritual ears according to Isaiah 50:4.

*"The Lord God has given Me
The tongue of the learned,
That I should know how to speak
A word in season to him who is weary.
He awakens Me morning by morning,
He awakens My ear
To hear as the learned.*

      ii. Pray and ask God to awaken your ears so that you can hear what He is saying to you.

  c. Spiritual heart

      i. We perceive things in our heart, which is the _____.

      ii. The Holy Spirit can cause feelings to come to you.

      iii. God will anoint your emotions, where you can _____ _____ and become touched with the infirmities of others in your heart.

RECEIVING FROM THE SPIRIT OF GOD

1. We receive from the spirit of God when we:

    a. _____

    b. _____

The Outpour

    c._____

2. The kingdom of God operates by _____.

Jesus is a greater leader than Satan is a deceiver!

3. The Holy Spirit will lead us to all truth when we ask Jesus for truth.

4. We can ask God for words of _____, _____, and _____

for believers.

PROPHESYING TO BELIEVERS

Prophecy for believers is released to:

1. Bless the body of Christ

   a. The first thing God does in Genesis 1:1 is to release _____.

   b. God is always ready to bless His people. We receive prophecy and prophesy by always looking for places of light and not of darkness.

2. Help us to focus

a. We _____ what the Holy Spirit and

God is saying to us.

b. Do daily activations to inquire of God's heart for you.

c. God is always speaking. We must _____,

_____, and began to

_____ to receive what He is saying!

3. Step into faith

Open your mouth wide, and I will fill it. ~ Psalm 81:10

a. Step out in _____ to release the one word or

picture God has given you and the river of prophecy will flow.

He who believes in Me, as the Scripture has said, out of his belly will flow rivers of living water." ~ John 7:38

b. The Greek would for river means _____ or

words. There are words that God is ready to release out of your belly.

But the manifestation of the Spirit is given to each one for the profit of all
~ 1 Corinthians 12:7

c. God has given each one of us a manifestation of the spirit. So we must fast, pray, and begin to believe that prophesying is our birthright given to us through Jesus.

4. End result

   a. End result is to put _____ and _____ back to mankind.

   b. Every time we speak it must put glory, honor, _____, _____, and bring _____

   c. God wants to _____!

Through our words we must be the generation that build up others and tear down the plans of the enemy!

THE PROPHETIC FLOW

*The spirit of a man is like the candle to the Lord,
Searching all the inner depths of his heart. ~ Proverbs 20:27*

1. The Spirit man is like the candle of the Lord, which God will light by _____ _____ to prophesy. You have to move in faith to speak those words out.

2. Prophecy and receiving prophecy do not always come in an audible voice, God speaks through your human spirit so it will sound like _____.

3. Pay attention to the voice of the Lord that is on the inside of you, God speak through your human spirit.

Keep your heart and your motives pure and God will speak to you!

GOD SPEAKS

1. Here are some ways you can begin to discern if God is speaking to you:

   a. Impressions are _____ or _____ to begin to speak what God is saying unto you.

   b. In a still small voice, we must quite ourselves down to receive what God is saying.

   c. Visions can be small _____ in your spirit man or they can be outside like a movie screen where God opens the heavenly realm to you for you to see clearly.

   d. Dreams are _____,

where God begins to speak to you clearly even on your bed (See Job 33).

e. Angelic visitations are one form of the outpouring of the glory realm.

Angels bring _____,

_____,

_____, and _____

from the throne of God and all we have to do is extend our faith to receive them.

f. Television is when you can see a news article or a story in media and it quickens something on the inside of us.

g. Preached messages are called _____
_____.

You are God's sheep, extend your faith and you will hear His voice and the voice of another you will not follow.

LESSON REFLECTIONS

After completing the video teachings, take a moment to reflect on the lesson using the following journal prompts.

1. Get into a quite place and ask the Lord what would you say to me today? What is on your heart for me today Lord? Then begin recording in your study guide what you hear God saying to you for the day.

2. What are the primary ways you hear the voice of God? Were you surprised by any of the ways that God speaks to us? Pray and ask the Holy Spirit to extend your faith so that you can hear God speak clearly.

3. As we cultivate hearing the voice of the Lord for ourselves, we can also grow in the ability to hear the voice of the Lord for others. Grab a partner and begin cultivating the voice of the Lord by listening and sharing with that person what God desires to communicate to him or her. Use the following activations to help you share God's voice with your partner.

Select one of the activations below. Take a moment to pray and ask God what to communicate to your partner concerning the topic. For example, image you selected the topic, "What color does your partner represent to God?" You would pray and ask, "God, what color does [insert partner's name] represent to You?" When you hear an answer, you would pray again and ask God, "Why? What does that mean?" Then you would share with the person what the Lord communicated to you. Now, choose one of the topics below and begin listening for God's voice.

   a. Ask God for a meaningful sentence for your partner. What does God want to communicate to your partner through this meaningful sentence?

   b. Ask God for a meaningful song for your partner. What does God want to communicate to your partner through this meaningful song?

   c. Ask God for areas He would like you to pray for concerning your partner. Why does God want you to pray for this particular area? What does He desire to communicate to your partner about this area?

Notes

The Outpour

LESSON 6

THE ROLE OF THE PROPHET IN THE LOCAL CHURCH

And God has appointed these in the church: first apostles, second prophets, third teachers, after that miracles, then gifts of healings, helps, administrations, varieties of tongues. ~ 1 Corinthians 12:28

Prophets are set in the local church to prophesy and stand next to others in the fivefold ministry. They are to move in their authority, to discern the heart and mind of God, and to help leadership in the local church move in a place of divine protection. In this lesson you will learn the:

- Reasons prophets are set in a church

- Roles prophets should serve in the local church

- Dimensions to delivering a prophetic word to a local church

- Tips for breaking through barriers to see revival in the local church

The Outpour

SET IN THE CHURCH

Fill in the blanks as you watch the video teachings to complete the lesson notes.

1. Prophets are set in the local church.

2. Set is a Greek word meaning to place, fix by appointment,

   _____ and authority, _____,

   to put in a certain place, post, position, or to set as a _____.

3. Prophets are set as a guard to the _____

   _____.

POSITIONS FOR PROPHETS IN THE CHURCH

1. Here are some positions that would benefit the local church if prophets occupied these positions:

   a. In the _____

   _____ where they can give

   direction, correction, help edify and build up the church.

   b. Prophets help confirm the _____

   _____ of leadership.

Then the prophet Haggai and Zechariah the son of Iddo, prophets, prophesied to the Jews who were in Judah and Jerusalem, in the name of the God of Israel, who was over them. So Zerubbabel the son of Shealtiel and Jeshua the son of Jozadak rose up and began to build the house of God which is in Jerusalem; and the prophets of God were with them, helping them.
~ Ezra 5:1-2

c. The prophet's ministry helps the body of Christ to move in _____

_____

_____ in their lives and

in the local church.

d. They unlock the _____

that the kingdom might be established and work can be finished.

e. Prophets help us to_____

_____. One of the dimensions of

the prophet's office is the office of the sons of Issachar.

Of the sons of Issachar who had understanding of the times, to know what Israel ought to do ~ 1 Chronicles 12:32

f. When we do not understand the times and the season, God will release

prophets to declare what time it is to the body of Christ.

g. The times and seasons of God can be released through

_____. Activation means to trigger and to stir

up. Prophets come to activate the heart and mind of God.

h. Prophets _____ through declarations what God is ready to do in a particular season of the church.

i. Prophets also impart where we need to learn to grow.

j. Prophets can also come to reiterate what we already know. When God sends a prophet, He is sending someone with His heart and His mind that has _____

_____

_____.

k. Prophets bring forth the word of God, because where the word of the Lord is there is power.

l. Prophets also_____, They should be set as watchman on the wall. Prophets should be part of the prayer team in the local assembly. They have the power and grace to pray until they see the power of God released in the local assembly.

i. God gives prophets an anointing, grace, and authority in the Spirit.

m. Prophets have the ability to release the grace of God and walk in

_____.

n. Prophets also have the ability to _____

_____ to the senior leadership.

o. God is releasing a grace for prophets to move forward to control the elements.

Foundations of Prophetic Ministry in the 21st Century

p. Prophets bring _____ and _____ the will of God, to go before God on behalf of the people and to go to the people on behalf of the God. This is a restoring of the spirit and power of Elijah being released on the earth, to keep praying with a great level of persistence.

BRINGING THE WORD OF GOD TO THE LOCAL CHURCH

1. When prophets bring the word of the Lord, the prophetic word must have four dimensions:

   a. Dimension of commendation

   "He who has an ear, let him hear what the Spirit says to the churches. To him who overcomes I will give to eat from the tree of life, which is in the midst of the Paradise of God." ' ~ Revelation 2:7

   i. Prophets must not get stuck looking for all the wrong things in the church.

   ii. Prophets must discern what is happening that is releasing the _____ .

   b. Understand the area where God wants to bring correction

i. One of the graces of the prophet's mantel is that you can _____, but you must be careful in how we deliver the word in the local church.

Jesus is our example as a prophet! He came with grace and truth.

c. Give instructions for correction

i. The ultimate goal as a prophet is to get people on the path of _____ and _____.

d. Show them the promise

i. Leave the church in the place of overcoming

PROPHETS OF BREAKTHROUGH AND REVIVAL

1. Prophets are a catalyst for _____.

2. Prophets have a grace and mantle on the inside of them to bring breakthrough

and deliverance.

3. Prophets are called to be _____ and to build the local church by placing and identifying the foundational stones of God Word as we release the spirit of _____.

4. The premier anointing on a prophet's life is the ability to walk with the _____.

5. Prophets have a grace to carry the presence of God.

6. God has released a creative force in your mouth, begin to create by speaking words of _____.

The essence of the prophet's office and prophecy is to bring life! Prophets bring the life of the Holy Spirit to a broken generation.

LESSON REFLECTIONS

After completing the video teachings, take a moment to reflect on the lesson using the following journal prompts.

1. How does your local church partner with prophets? How can you serve as an advocate to support the office of the prophet in your local church?

2. What do you create with your words? How can you be more intentional about speaking words of life over yourself, family, friends, community, and those who have offended you?

3. As we cultivate hearing the voice of the Lord for ourselves, we can also grow in the ability to hear the voice of the Lord for others. Grab a partner and begin cultivating the voice of the Lord by listening and sharing with that person what God desires to communicate to him or her. Use the following activations to help you share God's voice with your partner.

Select one of the activations below. Take a moment to pray and ask God what to communicate to your partner concerning the topic. For example, image you selected the topic, "What color does your partner represent to God?" You would pray and ask, "God, what color does [insert partner's name] represent to You?" When you hear an answer, you would pray again and ask God, "Why? What does that mean?" Then you would share with the person what the Lord communicated to you. Now, choose one of the topics below and begin listening for God's voice.

    a. Ask God for a meaningful number for your partner. What does God want to communicate to your partner through this meaningful number?

    b. Ask God for a corporate prophetic word for your partner's church. Be sure to incorporate all four dimensions for corporate prophetic words in the local church.

    c. Ask God for a meaningful connection between your partner and a current co-worker? What does God want to communicate to your partner about this co-worker?

Notes

The Outpour

ABOUT THE AUTHOR

Michelle McClain Walters is one of God's chosen Kingdom Prophets and she carries a strong apostolic spirit. There is a powerful, prophetic creative force in her mouth that sets lives on the course God originally ordained for them. Michelle cries loud and spares not. Her voice is an end of the age trumpet and also the voice of roaring lion, springing from the thickets, causing his prey to be petrified. The anointing on her life breaks the powers of darkness and sets the captives free, releasing them into a life of fruitfulness.

Michelle has traveled to over 50 nations and several cities in the U. S partnering with senior church leaders to release strategies that advance the Kingdom of God in their territory. She has conducted schools of the prophet that have activated thousands in the art of hearing the voice of God.

Michelle currently serves as Director of Prayer Ministry on the staff of Crusaders Church under the leadership of Apostle John Eckhardt. She is also one of the house prophets and apostolic team leaders at impact network. She is the Charisma House author of the Prophetic Advantage, the Prophetic Advantage Study Guide, The Esther Anointing, The Deborah Anointing, The Deborah Anointing Study Guide, The Anna Anointing, The Ruth Anointing, and Prayers and Declarations for the Woman of God.

Michelle resides in the city of Chicago along with her husband Pastor Floyd A Walters Jr.

LESSON

ANSWER KEY

Lesson 1: Prophetic Ministry in the 21st Century

Answer key for fill in the blanks.

GOD'S OUTPOURING

1. We serve a God who speaks __**to you**__ and __**through you**__.

2. God speaks in many ways, and this is our __**promise**__ and __**birthright**__.

3. A characteristic of the outpouring is that Gods want a people who is walking in __**obedience**__ to him to move in the same power Jesus walked in on earth.

4. This outpouring gives us access into the __**entire realm**__ of the Holy Spirit's activities.

5. This means that we can __**feel**__, __**know**__, and __**operate**__ in the same power Jesus operated in on earth.

The Outpour

6. The centerpiece of the outpouring of God's spirit is to **prophesy**.

7. If you are son and daughter (a believer of Jesus Christ) and filled with the Holy Spirit you are a **qualified** to operate in prophetic.

BIBLICAL FOUNDATION FOR PROPHECY

1. To move in the spirit of God we must come to a new place of **knowledge** and **understanding**.

    a. We don't operate in the gifts of the spirit because we are lacking knowledge about them.

    b. We have a responsibility as sons and daughters to have an understanding that **breaks the spirit of ignorance** and allows us to operate in the spirit of God.

2. All the gifts of the spirit operate by **love**, you need to understand how much God loves you and that He has a love for mankind.

    a. To operate in the fullness of everything God has for us, we have to start with a **desire**.

    b. Desire means to **have a longing for**, **to pursue**, and to go after something or someone..

    c. Prophecy is hearing the **heart** and the **mind of God** for your life, a situation, for your generation, your nation, and even for your city. God wants to reveal his heart and mind to us.

  d. Prophecy is a __**grace**__ given by the __**Holy Spirit**__ to hear the voice of God and release it to others.

  e. We release God's __**power**__ and __**presence**__ through prophecy.

3. The best gift of the Spirit is the __**gift that is needed at that time**__.

  a. Covet means to __**have a passion**__, lust after, __**to long**__ and yarn for.

  b. You can covet gift of prophecy.

4. Stir up the gifts of the Spirit by being __**convinced**__ that you at least have one of the giftsthe Spirit.

  a. Ask God to impart, activate, and __**release**__ the gift of prophecy on the inside of you.

  b. Pray and ask the Lord to __**fill**__ you with the knowledge of His will and the gift of prophecy.

  c. Come to some activations.

  d. The enemy wants to stop believers from operating in the fullness of the gifts of the spirit by attacking us with the spirit of fear; but God has given us a spirit of __**love**__, __**power**__, and __**sound mind**__.

5. Prophecy is given to the body of Christ to __**edify**__ the church.

The Outpour

    a.   Edify means to _**build up**_.

    b.   We have to seek, to go after, _**to look for**_, and to desire to prophesy.

    c.   We want to seek ways to bless the church, by being excellent in the gifts of prophecy and the gifts of the spirit.

6. With _**doubt**_ and _**unbelief**_, you can quench the spirit of God to move with the Spirit of God.

    a.   God is releasing faith on the inside of you.

7. The enemy can cause you to despise the gifts of the spirit.

    a.   Despise means to feel _**worthless**_, to reject, or to _**repeal**_.

    b.   Prophets and prophecy were God's ideas. He knew the misnomers and mistakes that would cause us to have the tendency to _**quench the spirit**_ and despise the gift of prophecy, but we can't throw the baby out with bathwater just because of mistakes.

8. Exercise and use the gifts becuase:

    a.   You can _**use**_ or _**lose**_ the gifts.

9. We neglect the gift of God by not _**studying**_ or partnering with a spirit of _**fear**_. We attend to the gifts of the spirit by:

    a.   Paying attention to the gifts and studying the God's word.

b. Taking every scripture you can find as it relates to prophets and prophecy and studying and meditating on them.

Pursue Prophecy

1. Christ **commands** us to pursue prophecy.

2. When we pursue prophecy it will bring great **joy to your life** .

3. Prophecy will cause you to draw near to God and to understand how much God loves you and the whole world.

Lesson 2: The Gift and Spirit of Prophecy

Answer key for fill in the blanks.

FOUNDATIONS TO THE PROPHETIC

1. The two natures or ways and expressions of prophecy is:

    a. Forthtelling which is __**speaking forth**__ the heart and mind of God.

    b. Foretelling which is to speak in a level of __**predicting**__, __**to announce**__, to communicate to the future, or to set agenda of God.

2. The three levels of prophetic ministry is the:

    a. Office of the prophet which is the __**highest level of ministry**__ and also the ministry of Jesus.

    b. Gift of prophecy which is the gift of the Holy Spirit __**resting on all believers**__.

    c. Spirit of prophesy which is created in an atmosphere of __**worship**__ where it is easy to prophecy in the local church.

OFFICE OF THE PROPHET

1. Prophets exist because we are still being __**perfected into the full measure of Jesus Christ**__.

2. Before Jesus ascended He took his mantle and separated it into five different

pieces know as the:

  a. Office of the ____**apostle**____

  b. Office of the ____**prophet**____

  c. Office of the evangelist

  d. Office of the ____**pastor**____

  e. Office of the teacher

3. It is a gift and calling from God to operate in one of these ____**fivefold**____ ascension gifts.

GIFT OF PROPHECY

1. The gift of prophecy is given by the ____**Holy Spirit**____ to those who desire it.

SPIRIT OF PROPHECY

1. The spirit of prophecy is when the ____**testimony of Jesus**____ is among believers.

2. When you come to worship gatherings the spirit of prophecy can rest upon you to ____**release the word of God**____.

FUNCTIONS OF THE OFFICE OF THE PROPHET

1. The functions of the office of the prophet is to provide __**direction**__ for the local church.

2. Prophets bring __**correction**__ and rebuke.

3. They have the ability to __**pronounce the divine decrees**__ of God's judgments or blessings.

4. Prophets move in strong level of __**revelation**__.

5. They move in the realm of illumination or __**present truth**__ of what God has to say to the church today.

6. Prophets lay the foundations in a church.

7. They __**impart**__ spiritual gifts.

GOD'S VIEW OF THE GIFT OF PROPHECY

1. We prophesy to __**edify**__ the church.

2. The gift of prophecy operates in three realms

    a. Edification

        i. Edify is an act of __**building up**__, to instruct, and to __**improve the mind of something**__, or to establish.

        ii. One of the dimensions of the prophetic realm is to __**build mankind up**__.

iii. Prophecy is a spiritual tool we can use through our words to bring edification to someone else.

b. Exhortation

i. Exhort means to call someone to move into action, __**to incite**__, __**to give life to**__, or to quicken too.

ii. Sometimes a word of exhortation can be a __**small rebuke**__.

iii. Holy Spirit on the inside of us is watching over our words to perform it

c. Comfort

i. Comfort means to __**relieve from pain**__, to ease, to uphold the mind of someone depressed, or to __**break confusion**__.

ii. Holy Spirit is known as the Comforter, He releases comfort by using vessels like us to speak words that will bring comfort to people.

For I know the thoughts that I think toward you, says the Lord, thoughts of peace and not of evil, to give you a future and a hope. ~ Jeremiah 29:11

3. When you begin moving in the realm of prophecy you begin releasing __**hope**__.

4. When you prophesy make sure you are releasing __**right words**__.

5. When moving in prophecy it is a realm of edification, exhortation, and comfort to God's people with His words in your mouth.

GOD'S VIEW OF THE SPIRIT OF PROPHECY

1. The greatest outpouring that God can release on a __**body of believers**__ simultaneously is the spirit of prophecy.

2. When the spirit of prophecy is in the atmosphere it:

    a. Turns your __**heart**__ and turns your __**nature**__.

    i. The spirit of prophecy is not resident. For example, when the spirit of prophecy came upon Saul it was not resident it was a __**grace**__ that came upon him from God.

    ii. When you minister to God in worship, the spirit of prophecy comes upon you. Saul received a __**tangible transfer**__ because of the spirit of prophecy. When he prophesied he turned into a new man.

    b. Prophesy turns our heart and the heart of others

3. The spirit of prophecy resting upon us as we worship is to bring __**healing**__ and __**deliverance**__.

4. We operate in the spirit of prophecy when we worship according to the portion of our __**faith**__.

Lesson 3: Identifying the Call of the Prophet

Answer key for fill in the blanks.

THE CALL OF GOD

1. The call of God is not like a __**menu**__, He call us before we were in our mother's womb.

2. Whatever you were called to do, when you came into your mother's womb God gave you __**everything you needed**__.

3. The call of God is given by the __**grace of God**__.

4. It is up to us to __**unlock**__ God's call by the power of God and by the Holy Spirit.

5. The prophet office is given to us before we were in our mother's womb

6. The call of God is an __**eternal call**__, started in the heart and mind of God and revealed by the Holy Spirit.

EXPECTATIONS OF THE CALL

1. God has an expectation for our lives and it is up to us to find it by getting before the __**presence of God**__.

2. We do not __**call**__, __**appoint**__, or __**set ourselves**__ over

anything – it is God who does the calling, setting, and appointing.

3. This does not mean we are rogue prophets and don't answer to anyone but God.

4. God sets prophets in the local **church** to be trained and commissioned.

DIMENSIONS IN A PROPHET'S DEVELOPMENT

There are three dimensions in a prophet's development.

1. The calling

    a. **A divine intervention** through an audible voice, a dream, or from other people who can identify the call of God in your life.

    b. Follow the draw and through the process of **identification**, God will identify you as a prophet.

2. God chooses the field where you are assigned.

    a. God is the one who gives you the **assignment** and **show** you where you are called.

    b. God who does the calling and chooses the prophet's assignment.

3. Appoints you to an office according to **His will** and **purpose** for your life.

    a. When God ordains you He gives you the unction, anointing, and authority to function.

b.　　Authority is the **legal right** or position to function.

c.　　God will develop the **servant** dimension in your life before you walk in the fullness of the office of the prophet.

d.　　He doesn't just give **revelation** and **impartation**. No, there is an unction and function that you have been assigned too, which means you need to be at the right place at the right time fulfilling the assignment of God.

e.　　We need to let God cultivate in us the desire for the place we are assigned

DEALS OF THE CALL

1. When you are being developed as a prophet, God will deal with the inadequacies or the **places you have fear or unworthiness**.

2. God will also deal with your **character** so that you have the capacity to carry out the call.

3. When God begins to speak to you about the call of God, He then **trains** and **commissions** you.

4. In the place of training, God will deal with your fears, insecurities, and your character, as He transforms you to carry out your assignment.

5. Fears try to eliminate our faith, therefore and we have to let the Lord begin to equip us and deliver us so that our faith can jump over our fears.

Your Message

1. God will develop your message so you don't have to ___**move out of your gifts**___.

2. Prophets bring messages of:

   a. ___**Righteousness**___

   b. ___**Repentance**___

   c. Glory

   d. ___**Healing**___ and ___**deliverance**___.

3. Prophets become confident and secure in the message that God has given them.

Your Vision

1. God will begin to recalibrate ___**your vision**___.

2. God will cause you to see ___**yourself**___ and ___**mankind**___ from His perspective.

3. Instead of looking from a low place or a human perspective, prophets are always called to go to the high place to see things from God's perspective.

4. Prophets were often called to a high place to have their vision recalibrated, to see mankind, to see their city, and their nation from God's perspective.

5. Prophets will go to high places with God in worship and there He will give them a

__heavenly perspective__.

COMMISSIONING

1. God wants to make you what **He wants you to be**.

2. The commissioning of God is a hard thing because we often don't see ourselves as

   God sees us.

3. If you have been called as prophet of the Lord you must be trained during

   long seasons with the Lord and then **commissioned** to be sent on

   assignment.

4. Credibility is not enough to hear the voice of God, we need **favor** with God

   and man.

   a. God wants to give you credibility so that people can honor you and trust you.

   When they trust you they will do what the word of the Lord is saying to do.

The Outpour

Lesson 4: Roadblocks to Accuracy

Answer key for fill in the blanks.

DIMENSION OF ACCURACY

1. We can have right words, but the wrong expression of God's heart.

2. Accuracy means to be __**correct**__, __**precise**__, and to have the __**correct expression**__.

3. To prophesy or to be a prophet is to speak the heart and mind of God.

4. The heart of God is the __**expression**__ or __**emotions**__ of God.

ROADBLOCKS TO ACCURATE DELIVERY

Things that can stop your accuracy with the delivery of prophetic words:

1. To opinionated

    a. We think our opinion is __**God's opinion**__.

    b. Don't speak your opinion.

    c. We stop speaking our opinions by seeking the Lord and not moving in __**presumption**__.

    d. Presumption is __**imitating the faith actions of others without**__

having the word of God quicken to your spirit.

   e. Avoid presumption by spending time with God!

2. Prejudice

   a. We cannot have racial, gender, and cultural prejudices or we will miss the accuracy of the prophetic.

   b. Make sure you have a **pure heart**.

   c. The **essence** of the prophetic ministry comes out of your heart.

3. Rejection and the fear of rejection

   a. Rejection or the fear of rejection will have you speaking words of prophecies to get **acceptance**.

   b. Ask the Lord to heal and deliver you from rejection and fear of rejection.

4. Fear of Man

   a. The Greek word for snare means **bait**, **lure**, or to put a ring in your nose.

   b. The fear of man will cause you to not prophesy without God's leading or to prophesy to **please** people.

5. Bitterness

   a. **Unresolved hurt** can lead to bitterness and taint our flow.

   b. Make sure you are not angry. The enemy attacks prophets because he

The Outpour

knows if he can get your heart, he can stop your accuracy.

6. Respecter of persons

   a. One of the dimensions of the prophet's office is likened to the high priest, who carried the breastplate with each jewel representing the twelve tribes of Israel.

   b. If you want to be accurate, you must be able to speak to the different tribes, **denominations** and even **cultures**, because God is a God of the nations and of every ethnic background, church, and denomination.

7. Human Compassion

   a. We must have compassion on what **God is judging**.

   b. Make sure you do not prophesy out of **your emotions**, always go for the right expression.

8. To judgmental

   a. The grace on the New Testament prophet's life is to **help**, not to point everything that is wrong.

9. Judging by appearance

   a. Don't look at someone's **appearance**.

   b. Ask the Lord what is on your heart and your mind for an individual.

   c. Don't let the appearance of someone **intimidate** you.

10. Lust

    a. Lust is having a **self-absorbed** desire for an object or a person.

b. Prophets must guard their hearts from the lust of **power**, **prestige**, and **promotion**.

TIPS TO FOLLOW

1. Have the right heart by desiring truth in your inmost parts by:

   a. **Praying** Psalm 51.

   b. Knowing the spirit of truth is the Holy spirit and He will give you truth.

2. Have a heart to immediately repentant because:

   a. Repentance makes it so that the wrong road will never become the right road.

      i. After repentance **rend your heart**.

      ii. Ask God if there is any evil way in you to purge it, and God will hear your prayer.

      iii. Allow the Holy Spirit to **search your heart**.

Lesson 5: Seek to Excel in Prophecy

Answer key for fill in the blanks.

RECEIVING PROPHETIC WORDS

1. Without the Holy spirit we have a **deficiency** to tap into and have greater understanding of the spiritual world.

2. We receive prophetic words though our senses. We have five natural senses just like we have five spiritual senses.

3. The way we catch prophecy is through our senses:

    a. Our spiritual eyes

        i. There is a dimension called the seer realm where we can **perceive things and pictures in our spirit by the Holy Ghost**.

        ii. The Holy Spirit will anoint your eyes like in 2 Kings 6 & 7 to see the things happening in the Spirit world that we cannot see with the naked eyes.

        iii. God can give you **pictures**, **dreams**, and **visions** by anointing you and removing spiritual scales from our eyes.

    b. Spiritual ears

i. God can open up our spiritual ears according to Isaiah 50:4.

   ii. Pray and ask God to awaken your ears so that you can hear what He is saying to you.

c. Spiritual heart

   i. We perceive things in our heart which is the **center of our being**.

   ii. The Holy Spirit can cause feelings to come to you.

   iii. God will anoint your emotions, where you can **feel what he is saying** and become touched with the infirmities of others in your heart.

RECEIVING FROM THE SPIRIT OF GOD

1. We receive from the spirit of God when we:

   a. **Ask**

   b. **Seek**

   c. **Knock**

2. The kingdom of God operates by **petition**.

3. The Holy Spirit will lead us to all truth when we ask Jesus for truth.

4. We can ask God for words of **edification**,

_____**exhortation**_____, and ___**comfort**_____ for believers.

PROPHESYING TO BELIEVERS

Prophecy for believers is released to:

1. Bless the body of Christ

    a. The first thing God does in Genesis 1:1 is to release ____**light**____.

    b. God is always ready to bless His people. We receive prophecy and prophesy by always looking for places of light and not of darkness.

2. Help us to focus

    a. We ____**perceive**____ what the Holy Spirit and God is saying to us.

    b. Do daily activations to inquire of God's heart for you.

    c. God is always speaking. We must ____**position our hearts**____, ____**open our ears**____, and began to ____**look in the spirit**____ to receive what He is saying!

3. Step into faith

    a. Step out in ____**faith**____ to release the one word or picture God has given you and the river of prophecy will flow.

    b. The Greek would for river means ____**rhetoric**____ or words. There are words that God is ready to release out of your belly.

    c. God has given each one of us a manifestation of the spirit. So we must fast, pray, and begin to believe that prophesying is our birthright given to us through Jesus.

4. End result

   a. End result is to put **glory** and **honor** back to mankind.

   b. Every time we speak it must put glory, honor, **validation**, **appreciation**, and bring **celebration**.

   c. God wants to **build us and others**!

THE PROPHETIC FLOW

1. The Spirit man is like the candle of the Lord, which God will light by **dropping words in your spirit** to prophesy. You have to move in faith to speak those words out.

2. Prophecy and receiving prophecy do not always come in an audible voice, God speaks through your human spirit so it will sound **like you**.

3. Pay attention to the voice of the Lord that is on the inside of you, God speak through your human spirit.

GOD SPEAKS

1. Here are some ways you can begin to discern if God is speaking to you:

    a. Impressions are **slight nudges** or **slight unctions** to begin to speak what God is saying unto you.

    b. In a still small voice we must quite ourselves down to receive what God is saying.

    c. Visions can be small **pictures** in your spirit man or they can be outside like a movie screen where God opens the heavenly realm to you for you to see clearly.

    d. Dreams are **parables in the night**, where God begins to speak to you clearly even on your bed (See Job 33).

    e. Angelic visitations are one form of the outpouring of the glory realm.. Angels bring **healing**, **deliverance**, **restoration**, and **messages** from the throne of God and all we have to do is extend our faith to receive them.

    f. Television is when you can see a news article or a story in media and it quickens something on the inside of us.

    g. Preached messages are called **prophetic preaching**.

Foundations of Prophetic Ministry in the 21st Century

Lesson 6: The Role of the Prophet in the Local Church

Answer key for fill in the blanks.

SET IN THE CHURCH

1. Prophets are set in the local church.

2. Set is a Greek word meaning to place, fix by appointment, **agreement** and authority, **to arrange**, to put in a certain place, post, position, or to set as a **guard**.

3. Prophets are set as a guard to the **body of Christ**.

POSITIONS FOR PROPHETS IN THE CHURCH

1. Here are some positions that would benefit the local church if prophets occupied these positions:

    a. In the **leadership or government of the church** where they can give direction, correction, help edify and build up the church.

    b. Prophets help confirm the **mission and plans** of

leadership.

c. The prophet's ministry helps the body of Christ to move in _____**faith and courage to fulfill the assignment of God**_____ in their lives and in the local church.

d. They unlock the _____**realm of prosperity**_____ that the kingdom might be established and work can be finished.

e. Prophets help us to_____**discern the times and season of God**_____. One of the dimensions of the prophet's office is the office of the sons of Issachar.

f. When we do not understand the times and the season, God will release prophets to declare what time it is to the body of Christ.

g. The times and seasons of God can be released through _____**activations**_____. Activation means to trigger and to stir up. Prophets come to activate the heart and mind of God.

h. Prophets _____**announce**_____ through declarations what God is ready to do in a particular season of the church.

i. Prophets also impart where we need to learn to grow.

j. Prophets can also come to reiterate what we already know. When God sends a prophets, He is sending someone with His heart and His mind that has _____**the power to perform the announcement**_____.

k. Prophets bring forth the word of God, because where the word of the Lord is there is power.

l.   Prophets also **protect**. They should be set as watchman on the wall. Prophets should be part of the prayer team in a local assembly. They have the power and grace to pray until they see the power of God released in the local assembly.

i.   God gives prophets an anointing, grace, and authority in the Spirit.

m.   Prophets have the ability to release the grace of God and walk in **right times and right seasons**.

n.   Prophets also have the ability to **bring words of edification** to the senior leadership.

o.   God is releasing a grace for prophets to move forward to control the elements

p.   Prophets bring **intercession** and **birth forth** the will of God, to go before God on behalf of the people and to go to the people on behalf of the God. This is a restoring of the spirit and power of Elijah being released on the earth, to keep praying with a great level of persistence.

BRINGING THE WORD OF GOD TO THE LOCAL CHURCH

1. When prophets bring the word of the Lord, the prophetic word must have four dimensions:

a. Dimension of commendation

   i. Prophets must not get stuck looking for all the wrong things in the church.

   ii. Prophets must discern what is happening that is releasing the **goodness and the grace of God**.

b. Understand the area where God wants to bring correction

   i. One of the graces of the prophet's mantel is that you can **see what the enemy is doing**, but you must be careful in how we deliver the word in the local church.

c. Give instructions for correction

   i. The ultimate goal as a prophet is to get people on the path of **righteousness** and **doing the will of God**.

d. Show them the promise

   i. Leave the church in the place of overcoming

PROPHETS OF BREAKTHROUGH AND REVIVAL

1. Prophets are a catalyst for **bringing forth breakthrough and revival**.

2. Prophets have a grace and mantle on the inside of them to bring breakthrough

and deliverance

3. Prophets are called to be __**builders**__ and to build the local church by placing and identifying the foundational stones of God's Word as we release the spirit of __**acceptance**__.

4. The premier anointing on a prophet's life is the ability to walk with the __**spirit of the fear of the Lord**__.

5. Prophets have a grace to carry the presence of God

6. God has released a creative force in your mouth, begin to create by speaking words of __**life**__.

Made in the USA
Monee, IL
06 December 2020